PUPPETRY

PUPPETRY

A guide for beginners

Marie Kruger

CAPE TOWN

Dedicated to Doeks van Niekerk who
taught and inspired me

Delos, 40 Heerengracht, Cape Town

© 1990 Delos
Also available in Afrikaans as : Poppespel: 'n gids vir beginners
Translated by Rosalind Goodman
Photography by Colin Elliott
Illustrations by Anne Westoby
Cover design by Abie and Jasmine Fakier
Book design by Tina-Marié Malherbe
Set in 10½ on 12 point Palatino Roman by McManus Bros.,
Cape Town
Printed and bound by National Book Printers, Goodwood, Cape
First edition, first print 1990

ISBN 1-86826-105-0

The two life-sized rod puppets on the previous page (with shoulder-
pieces and sophisticated central control rods) on the previous page
have exaggerated, caricatured features. They perform in an open
acting space. The puppeteers are dressed in black.
(Made by Doeks van Niekerk)

Contents

Introduction

For centuries, puppets have fascinated both young and old in every part of the world. The pleasure of puppetry lies not only in the enjoyment it gives an audience, but also in the satisfaction obtained by the puppeteer in working creatively with elements of other art forms.

As with every other art form, puppetry relies very heavily on a creative imagination. That is why this book provides no quick-and-easy patterns or texts. Given some suggestions and construction methods, you will be able to discover the basic techniques for yourself and then test your own creative powers.

Before you rush off and start making puppets, it is essential first to reflect on exactly what a puppet is and how it differs from its living counterpart – if such a creature of the imagination could actually be said to have a counterpart. To prevent your making a puppet and then not knowing what to do with it, let's look first at a number of ideas about puppets. Afterwards, you can make a puppet and discover how to bring it to life in its own distinctive world.

Unlike an ordinary doll, the puppet is an extension of the puppeteer: one doesn't talk *to* it as one does to a doll, one talks *through* it in order to communicate with an audience. In the process, it is not only the audience that is entertained and enriched: the puppeteer too, however inexperienced, enjoys the pleasure of fantasy becoming reality and a reality about which he can fantasize freely. For this reason puppetry, although a versatile art form, is accessible even to a child.

This old man (modelling-clay base) needs two manipulators: one for the moveable mouth and neck, and a second to work the hands. The rats are three simple figures on a central control rod. (Made by Doeks van Niekerk)

CHAPTER 1

The puppet

Puppets are found in a variety of forms, e.g. glove puppets, rod puppets, marionettes, finger puppets, flat figures (like shadow puppets and Jumping Jacks) and even puppets controlled by the feet. Puppets can therefore be two- or three-dimensional, be manipulated from various different positions (above, below, behind, from the sides) and differ from each other in size. The puppet is, however, always an inanimate (i.e. lifeless) object which must be brought to life by a person.

To create the impression that a puppet is alive, it must be able to move. And it is precisely in this regard that we find the greatest difference between a puppet and a doll: the limbs of the puppet are looser so that it can move easily. It is made in such a way that the puppeteer can move certain parts, for example the head, arms and hands, using his own hand, which is invisible to the audience.

Speech or singing also gives the illusion of life to a puppet, but movement gives the audience a greater conviction that the puppet is alive because one is more strongly influenced by what one sees than by what one hears.

When you make a puppet and tell a story or present a little play with it, it is important to remember that it is not a miniature person or animal. Therefore it does not have to be a realistic imitation. It is a fantasy figure which has grown out of someone's imagination and creativity.

Instead of being a faithful reproduction, it is rather more a symbol of a certain type of person or animal with only a few very distinct characteristics. So, for example, it will be good or bad, friendly or surly, stupid or clever. A good puppet's character and emotions must first show in its appearance and then be confirmed and reinforced by the way it moves and speaks. Unlike an ordinary actor, the puppet cannot present a variety of characters with dissimilar characteristics. The kindly king can never become a pitiful begger, for instance, nor the wicked witch a friendly grandmother.

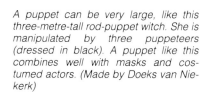

A puppet can be very large, like this three-metre-tall rod-puppet witch. She is manipulated by three puppeteers (dressed in black). A puppet like this combines well with masks and costumed actors. (Made by Doeks van Niekerk)

To sum up, then, the puppet is:

- *a lifeless object which is brought to life by a puppeteer using movement and speech*

- *not an ordinary doll*

- *an expression of fantasy*

- *not a miniature person or animal*

- *a simplification and an expression of the imagination*

- *a symbol, not a realistic imitation of reality*

11

CHAPTER 2

Ways of using the puppet

Ancient Western peoples used the puppet as a part of sacred rituals. By 400 B.C., puppet theatre was an established form of entertainment for adults. Performances were often given in public places like parks, on street corners and at fairs. Since 1950 it has been a popular children's entertainment. In the field of education, puppets are today a popular teaching aid and stimulus to learning.

Two aspects must, however, always be kept in mind:

- *The puppet wants to entertain even when someone is being taught something, and*
- *The puppet can entertain people of any age group.*

It is a misconception to think of it as only suited to entertaining small children. It can be used to advantage by children, parents, teachers, librarians, museologists, speech therapists, occupational therapists, entertainers or anyone in whom there is a spark of imagination begging to be let out.

When puppet theatre is presented with entertainment as its only, or chief, goal it is still never without educational merit. Both audience and puppeteer are spiritually, culturally and intellectually enriched while enjoying a wholesome form of relaxation.

As a teaching aid a puppet can convey any facts in any subject. The teacher can be the puppeteer, but it is sometimes more successful if the child himself handles the puppet. This always enhances the learning process because it is active and concrete, and the child's interest is stimulated. Owing to the visual impact of puppetry, children who are not actively involved always listen more attentively. At the same time the teacher, with the necessary planning, can cover the syllabus in an integrated project.

As part of the language study programme, the puppet can improve the child's writing, spelling and speaking abilities in an enjoyable way while the teacher unobtrusively participates as language model.

A withdrawn child is encouraged to speak more willingly by creating a sympathetic space for him when he stands behind a screen, forgets about himself and identifies with his puppet. In this way the teacher can identify possible language, learning and emotional problems. So puppetry can serve as a diagnostic aid by means of which the child's ideas, feelings and experiences can be simultaneously determined. This leads to a better understanding of the child as a person.

By means of puppetry, children can be helped to solve their social, emotional and personal problems or resolve any conflict. Healthy behaviour patterns can be established in an enjoyable way. To use this potential in the puppet to full advantage, children must get the opportunity to create a text and manipulate the puppets themselves under the guidance of the teacher.

Puppetry has been practised for centuries as a solo activity. It is also an enjoyable group activity which develops social bonds and in which each individual can employ his special talent in the creation of a text, the design and making of puppets and décor, and the performance of the text by means of movement, speech, singing and even sound effects and lighting.

To sum up, the puppet is used:

- *always to entertain*
- *to convey factual information*
- *to make the learning process active and concrete*
- *to make language teaching enjoyable*
- *to increase the self-confidence of the performer*
- *to stimulate social and emotional growth*

CHAPTER 3

The text of the puppet play

Published texts for the puppet theatre are often difficult to obtain and do not always conform to the needs of a specific group of performers. A good published text is, however, a valuable starting point for inexperienced adults, who can learn the potential of puppets and the basic principles of puppetry from these texts. They serve as a point of departure for original texts and adaptations.

Children must be allowed to create their own text under the guidance of an experienced adult. In the case of older pupils, the text can eventually be written down word for word. Apart from one's own original text, existing fairy-tales, folk legends, myths and fables can be adapted for use as a puppet play.

To be successful, a text should always conform to certain basic requirements which are determined by the principles on which puppet theatre is based, namely:

- *movement*
- *strong characterization*
- *simplicity*
- *exaggeration*
- *fantasy*
- *imaginativeness*

General textual requirements

Like any dramatic text, a puppet play must have dramatic action, i.e. actions (physical movement), ideas, emotions (which flow from certain actions and motivate yet others) and dialogue.

Action and dialogue

For the puppet, movement is the most important form of dramatic action because it best creates the illusion of life. A puppet which only speaks does not convince an audience and will soon lead to boredom. The emotions and ideas of the puppet must as far as possible be shown by movement, even if it is as limited a movement as the turning away of a face or the wave of a hand. If the puppet is shy it could, for example, go and stand in a corner, cover its face with its hands, turn away from the audience and bow its head. Even if it then said nothing at all, the audience could deduce from its behaviour how it felt. In this way a whole story could be told with movement alone.

Movement can, however, be supported by dialogue.

Dialogue helps to clarify the theme or main idea of the puppet play, unfold the plot (the plan of the action) and make the characteristics of the different characters clear to the audience, not only from what they do but also from what they say and what others say about them.

In a good puppet play the dialogue is always subordinate to the action. This does not mean that dialogue is superfluous; it is simply a less convincing way of giving life to a character than movement – especially if the puppet does not have a moveable mouth. Long speeches unaccompanied by action should be avoided. They result in a static quality which destroys the fantasy world and liveliness of the puppet.

Ensure that the visual image remains lively and supplement it with dialogue, music or even conventional story-telling. If dialogue is replaced by the latter this must not, however, detract from the dramatic quality of the puppet play.

Movement, simplicity and imaginativeness

Because the puppet play tells the story chiefly through

13

movement, the action must be clear and comprehensible. It must be simple, but at the same time imaginative. This combination links puppetry strongly with mime, an art form which relies on simplicity in order to be understood. Simplicity should not, however, be confused with monotony. Imaginative simplicity is always absorbing, entertaining and comprehensible. Even a text intended to convey certain educational ideas and principles to an audience should always entertain because this remains the main objective of puppet theatre.

Characterization, simplicity and exaggeration

The text must also provide for simplicity in characterization. A puppet is always a symbol, i.e. a simplification of reality. Therefore it has a less complex character than a real person. Its few characteristics have already been built into its appearance (i.e. construction) and strongly emphasized, even exaggerated. These characteristics must be further illustrated in the text by what it does and says. Strong characterization always leads to clear understanding on the part of the audience.

The simplified yet strong character of a puppet in a play should always be kept in mind in the choice of conflict in the text. Conflict leads to dramatic action, especially in the form of emotions and events. Even when children – with or without puppets – improvise, conflict quickly develops in the situation they are acting out. Children often

sense instinctively that there must be conflict or a problem which is then resolved in order to create an interesting situation.

A puppet cannot, however, easily undergo a character change. Its character should already be visible in its appearance. Only puppets which are made from soft material such as cloth and foam rubber and have moveable mouths can to a certain extent change the expression of emotion on their faces. Subtle and complicated emotions, as well as altered emotional states which cannot be expressed through movement and posture, should preferably be avoided.

The conflict in the text should therefore not lead to a character transformation, but rather follow the age-old fairy-tale pattern according to which good and evil are in conflict and the good finally triumphs. In this way the audience's trust in the good is confirmed and strengthened.

The type of puppet and its text

The events in a text must at all times be suited to adequate performance by puppets. Each type of puppet possesses inherent characteristics and ways of moving, so all puppets are not suited to all texts, and vice versa.

If you wish to use a specific type of puppet, e.g. a glove puppet, create a text which makes provision for the possibilities and limitations of this particular type. If you produce a text without a definite type of puppet in mind, you will have to consider carefully in

performing the text what type of puppet will present it best. If necessary, the action should be adapted slightly.

A text for the ordinary glove puppet, the glove puppet with a moveable mouth, and the finger puppet must make provision for the inherent comic quality of these puppets. For a serious text or character the dignified rod puppet or marionette would be a better choice. (As a versatile medium of expression the rod puppet and marionette do, however, also lend themselves to the interpretation of comic situations.) Unlike the ordinary glove puppet, the rod puppet and marionette cannot handle props, however. If a text requires the use of props, the ordinary glove puppet is definitely the best choice.

For finger puppets simple, short, comic situations or rhymes, short poems and songs which can be presented in visually dramatic terms could be chosen for an intimate audience. They can also be used with glove and rod puppets in a story to represent a very small person or animal.

When you create a text for shadow puppets, keep their non-realistic nature in mind. Look for supernatural, mystical or fantastic events and use story-telling or music in place of dialogue. It is also possible to enact certain scenes in a glove or rod puppet play with shadow puppets if you set up a light source behind a suitable screen (a taut bed sheet or even thick tracing paper) in the acting areas.

A text for ordinary flat figures must reckon with the limited potential for movement of these puppets, which only have a front and a side

view. Events therefore take on a tableau-like quality and chiefly consist of the figures being moved past each other (as for instance in the well-known story of the three billy-goats gruff and the wicked troll). Flat figures can sometimes be used with glove puppets and rod puppets to represent tableau movements, especially of large crowds. A number of figures can then be attached to one rod. One puppeteer can even handle two groups of flat figures at the same time. In this way a crowd scene can be presented with fewer puppeteers and in a smaller acting area.

The text and fantasy

The action in a text must not only be suited to being performed by puppets, but be presented *more* effectively by puppets than by living actors. For this reason, the puppet theatre often uses fantasy characters and events. Some events which would be difficult to present on the living stage make outstanding ideas for the puppet, which lives in a world in which fantasy is a reality and in which one can fantasize about reality.

Rumpelstiltskin (e.g. a glove puppet) disappears through the floor in rage without a trapdoor having to open beneath him, simply by having the puppeteer drop his arm quickly below the acting area. Cinderella can appear instantly in her beautiful ballgown without any difficulty if two separate puppets are made: the fairy godmother waves her wand, a clash of cymbals follows, the puppeteer quickly drops the hand with the ragged Cinderella on it and raises the other hand to reveal the beautiful Cinderella.

Not only fairy-tale events and characters can be presented better and more easily with puppets, however. Ani-

In this performance of The Three Billy-goats Gruff, *a glove puppet with freely hanging legs (the troll) is combined with flat figures (the billy-goats), cut from cardboard and decorated with cloth, paint, string and buttons. (Made by Marie Kruger)*

mal characters are in general more convincing if they are represented by puppets. Even certain everyday events, for example a motor accident, can be more easily portrayed by puppets.

The length of the text

In creating a text you must think carefully about the number of scenes and the length of the text. The audience must be entertained and their attention held throughout. So take the attention span of your audience into account: the younger the audience, the shorter the text. Always remember that puppetry is a

A performance of Puss in Boots, *a fairytale with enough action for a puppet play. (Coach and puppets made by Doeks van Niekerk)*

concentrated form of theatre and the enjoyment thereof demands a more intense experience from the audience than an ordinary play does. Be brief, but comprehensible and imaginative. Try to present events in a limited number of scenes with the minimum number of scene changes, rapidly achieved. Too many scenes together with a change of locale interrupts the flow and suspense and cannot hold the audience's attention all through the play.

So always aim for:

Action

- *which tells the whole story,*
- *is performable,*
- *is simple, imaginative and entertaining and*
- *reveals the characters of the puppets in the play.*

Dialogue

- *which supports the action,*
- *is typical of a particular character,*
- *and is brief and stimulating.*

Characterization

- *which is strong and clear,*
- *can be exaggerated, and*
- *has been simplified into a few characteristics.*

Keep the following factors in mind in creating a text:
- *purpose of the performance*
- *age of the audience*
- *skill of the puppeteers*
- *number of puppeteers available*
- *acting facilities available*

Ideas for a puppet play text

The creation of a text for a puppet play is a creative process, so no hard-and-fast rules can be laid down for a working method. I therefore give no plot or story outlines, only a number of hints.

Hints for adaptations

- *Choose a fairy-tale, myth, folk legend or fable which contains sufficient performable action.*
- *Ensure that the events, movements, emotions and conflict can be presented by puppets. Simplify, replace or omit events which are difficult to represent.*
- *Choose a story in which the characters are types rather than individuals with complex emotions.*
- *Always keep the leading characters in the play right to the end. For a more concise text which is easier to perform, you can leave out less important characters and give their dramatic function to other characters.*
- *Eliminate sub-plots and retain only the main events of the story.*
- *Cut out any unnecessary repetition of events.*
- *Combine and/or rearrange scenes to avoid too much interruption of time and place.*
- *In a story, the background of the narrative is often dealt with at length. Retain only the essential information and, in the form of concise dialogue, weave it into what is happening here and now.*
- *Bring the puppet play to an end when the problem is solved.*

Hints for a puppet play text by children

- *Let each child make a puppet of his own choice.*
- *Divide the puppets into groups, e.g. people, animals, fantasy figures, or according to style (size of puppets, similarity in colour, or degree of detail). Puppets which do not belong to a distinctive group can be divided among the other groups and perhaps give rise to the idea of a story, in this way providing the conflict.*
- *Each child decides on the gender, name, age and characteristics of his puppet. He must be allowed to adapt these initial ideas.*
- *Questions about locale can serve as the stimulus for the development of a story, e.g. where are the characters, do they all live together, do they like it there? Fantasy places can be used and will often provide the conflict, e.g. a cave, a remote island, a dense forest or a strange planet.*
- *A hero or heroine can be chosen in order to provide a story with dramatic qualities. After doing so, ask the group questions such as: what is his/her problem, how can the problem be solved? After this, another hero/heroine is chosen and the same questions are asked. Then the group make a final choice.*
- *Once the group have decided on an idea, they act it out. The teacher and members of the group can make suggestions to improve the puppet show. When a group feels ready, they can perform the story with another group as audience.*

Hints for an original text

- *Think in terms of action. Create the text, therefore, by means of a series of events.*
- *Consider the conflict: who is concerned in it, what are their relationships to each other,*

18

These three glove puppets show the fantasy nature of the puppet: reality and imagination are combined. (Made by education students, U.S.)

Hints for an educational text

- *Choose a subject which is of topical interest to the audience.*
- *Interweave the educational objective with an entertaining story.*
- *Do not become obviously didactic or preach at your audience. Lead them to the proper insight through the events of the play.*
- *Supplement the educational content with humour, interesting action and scenes which lead up to an appropriate climax.*
- *Plan the events so that audience participation becomes possible. Participation from the audience will help the educational aims of the play to catch on.*
- *The dialogue should be simple and direct and the speeches short. Pantomime can sometimes be used in place of dialogue.*
- *Make sure that the puppet play stays exciting and full of surprises and that the audience remains entertained throughout.*
- *The audience should leave after the performance with a feeling of excitement, and with sympathy for the good characters. They must never feel that they have just sat through a sermon.*

Both children and adults can use the above hints. Older children and adults can, if they choose, write the dialogue down either in broad outline or word for word. In the latter case, they should always leave room for changes in response to audience reaction.

how will the problem be solved? Everything leads up to the climax.
- *Think about each character: what are its characteristics, what is its function?*
- *Ensure that the climax of the action evokes a positive reaction in the audience.*
- *Consider whether the action can be performed by puppets and what type you will use.*
- *Divide the events into scenes.*
- *Find appropriate dialogue. It can be written down word for word, or only indicated in broad outline, or remain unwritten.*

CHAPTER 4

How to make a puppet

Making a puppet is a creative process in which provision should be made for the maker's own initiative and imagination. Instead of exact patterns, a number of construction methods are given here which are simple enough for beginners and which can be adapted by more experienced people to make a more complicated puppet.

GLOVE PUPPETS

The glove puppet consists of a head, a small cylinder which forms the neck and a sock (the body and costume), to which are attached two hands. Sometimes two legs hanging freely from the sock are attached to the front. Some glove puppets, often animal characters, have a moveable mouth. We thus distinguish between the ordinary glove puppet (without a moveable mouth) and the glove puppet with a moveable mouth. mouth.

Ordinary glove puppets

The head

This part is made first. (See fig. 1, p. 21 for the correct proportions for a human head.) These proportions can be adjusted (eyes close together, nose very large) for strong characterization.

Ball head

- Use a ball (rubber ball, tennis ball) and cut a cross in it using a sharp knife (see fig. 2, p. 21).
- Use thick cardboard to make a neck cylinder wide enough to fit over the index finger and long enough to reach the top of the head on the inside. The lower end should fit just above the second joint of the index finger.
- Apply paste or glue to the

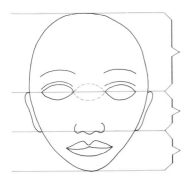

Figure 1:

Proportions of the human head: the top of the ears is in line with the eyes, the bottom of the ears is in line with the tip of the nose, and the eyes are one eyewidth apart.

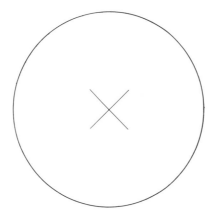

Figure 2:

Cut a cross in the ball with a sharp instrument.

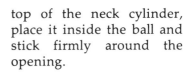

top of the neck cylinder, place it inside the ball and stick firmly around the opening.

Decoration

Paint the ball and neck cylinder if they are not the desired colour. Allow to dry. Provide the head with eyes, a nose and a mouth, using paint or other materials like felt (eyes, nose) or a cork (nose). Stick on hair (wool, string, raffia, ribbon or strips of cloth).

Many stories about the Jackal and the Wolf (here seen with Wolf's wife) make entertaining puppet plays. The house is made from a cardboard box and the heads of the glove puppets are modelled round a balloon (see p. 22). (Made by Marie Kruger)

21

Head with balloon base

- Blow up a small, round balloon to the approximate size of a tennis ball.
- Tie it up tightly and hold it under water in a container to ensure that no air is escaping in the form of bubbles.
- Prepare starch as follows: Put one tablespoon (15 ml) of starch into a container and mix with half a tablespoon (7,5 ml) of cold water to form a smooth paste. Gradually add 1¼ cups (312 ml) freshly boiled water to the mixture, stirring constantly. When the starch is ready it will have a transparent quality. Allow to cool.
- Cover the working surface with newspaper.
- Taking half a sheet of newspaper at a time, use your hand to apply starch to both sides of the paper. The starched paper should look transparent. Remove all excess starch.
- Tear off small pieces of the starched paper and stick at least four overlapping layers over the balloon. If you use printed and blank newspaper alternately, you will be able to distinguish between the layers easily.
- If necessary, the nose, cheeks, chin and mouth can be built up with small pieces of starched paper.
- Allow to dry thoroughly.
- Provide with a neck cylinder (see ball head, p. 20).

Decoration

Paint the face and features. The eyes, mouth and nose can also be stuck on. Attach hair (see ball head, p. 20). Make a beard and/

or a moustache of the same material as the hair.

Head with modelling-clay base

- Form the desired head and features from modelling clay.
- Place a neck cylinder (see ball head, p. 20) in the clay base.
- Coat the clay base with petroleum jelly.
- Stick starched newspaper all over the clay base (see balloon base, p. 22). Do not cover the neck cylinder, and remove it as soon as

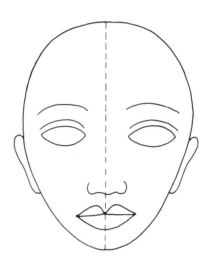

Figure 3:

Cut the paper covering vertically in two.

you have finished sticking newspaper on the head.
- Allow to dry.
- Cut the paper casing through vertically using a sharp knife (see fig. 3, p. 22). Remove all clay.
- Join the two halves with paste or glue. Cover the join with another layer of starched newspaper.

- Put the neck cylinder back and attach with paste or glue. To strengthen it, cover the neck cylinder with starched paper where the neck and head meet as well.

Decoration

Paint the face, eyes and mouth. Attach hair (see ball head, p. 20).

Bluebeard the Wizard (balloon base) with a painted ice-cream cone as a hat, button eyes and string hair with the Green Witch (modelling-clay base) and the Grey Witch (crumpled newspaper base) – see p. 22 and 24 for construction methods. (Made by drama students, U.S.)

HEAD MADE FROM CLOTH

Round face (See fig. 4, p. 24)

- Choose cloth with a colour (not necessarily realistic) and texture approriate for the character.
- Cut two circles 8,9 cm in diameter.
- Cut a long strip 3,2 cm x 24,1 cm out of the same cloth.
- Stitch the strip to the two circles. Leave an opening for the neck cylinder.
- Stuff the head lightly with any suitable material (small pieces of foam rubber, cotton wool, cut-up nylon stockings).
- Make a neck cylinder out of thick cardboard big enough to fit over the index finger (see ball head, p. 20).
- Stick a strip of cloth over the cylinder.
- Sew the cylinder firmly to the head.

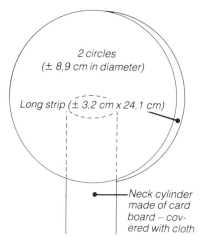

2 circles
(± 8,9 cm in diameter)

Long strip (± 3,2 cm x 24,1 cm)

Neck cylinder made of cardboard – covered with cloth

Figure 4:

Round face made of cloth: 2 circles, 1 long strip, neck cylinder

Decoration

Embroider or stick on eyes, nose

---

and mouth. Make ears from the same kind of material (a double layer) with the inside layer a contrasting colour if desired. Sew the ears firmly to the head on the long strip.

Head with crumpled newspaper base

- Crumple dry newspaper to obtain the desired shape for the head (e.g. round or oval, without features).
- Place the newspaper base on a bottle with a narrowish neck (e.g. a wine bottle).
- Take a piece of dry newspaper. Fold it over the newspaper base and the neck of the bottle. Stick it down around the neck of the bottle with sticky tape.
- Prepare some starch (see balloon base, p. 22). Spread both sides of a piece of newspaper with starch.
- Stick at least four overlapping layers of starched newspaper over the head and neck.
- Model the features (eye sockets, nose, cheeks, chin, mouth) with compressed starched paper. Stick small pieces of starched paper over the features.
- Allow to dry.
- Remove the bottle.
- Scrape all loose newspaper out of the inside of the head through the neck opening.
- If the neck is too wide, it can be made narrower with starched paper or foam rubber.

Decoration

Paint the head, neck and features. Attach hair (see ball head, p. 20) and a beard and/or moustache if necessary.

Stocking head

- Take a stocking of suitable colour and stuff it lightly with any suitable material (small pieces of foam rubber, cotton wool, cut-up nylon stockings).
- Make a neck cylinder from thick cardboard to fit over the index finger (see ball head, p. 20).
- Place the neck cylinder inside the head and tie firmly with string.
- Paste or glue a part of the stocking over the neck cylinder and cut off the excess stocking.

Decoration

Embroider or stick on features such as mouth, nose, eyes and cheeks. Embroider or stick on hair (see ball head, p. 20), as well as a beard and/or moustache if desired.

Oval face (See fig. 5, p. 25)

Use the same method as for a round face, but cut two oval sections (8,3 cm x 10,2 cm) and a long strip 3,2 cm x 28 cm.

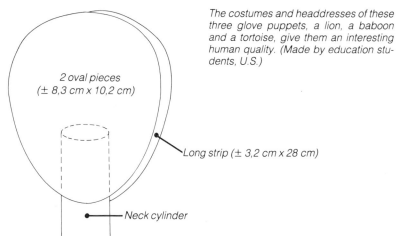

2 oval pieces
(± 8,3 cm x 10,2 cm)

Long strip (± 3,2 cm x 28 cm)

Neck cylinder

Figure 5:

Oval face made of cloth: 2 oval pieces, 1 long strip, neck cylinder

The costumes and headdresses of these three glove puppets, a lion, a baboon and a tortoise, give them an interesting human quality. (Made by education students, U.S.)

25

The glove puppet's costume

The costume should fit comfortably over the hand of the puppeteer and cover the whole forearm. The puppeteer must have control over the glove puppet's hands in order to make appropriate gestures and pick up props (basket, book, axe, etc.). The colour, texture and general appearance of the costume should support the strong characterization of the puppet in the play. In the case of animal characters the colour of the face, costume (body) and hands (forefeet) usually blends together. An animal character can wear a hat, coat, jacket, tie, waistcoat, cloak, etc., just like a human character.

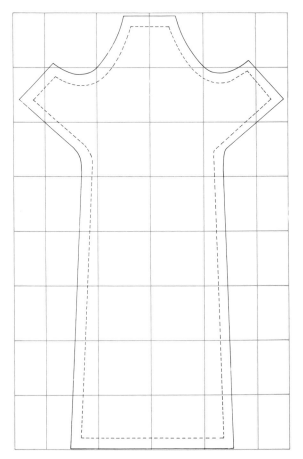

Figure 6:

Underskirt (body) for glove puppet
Do not stitch the neck and the bottom edge closed. Stitch the sleeves closed if you wish to add hands.
Size: adult's hand

Costume for glove puppet without legs

- Make a petticoat (body) out of simple material such as unbleached calico, according to fig. 6 on p. 26.
- Attach the body to the neck just below the head using paste, glue or thread.
- Make a costume that fits over the body according to the same pattern (see fig. 6, p. 26), with variations where needed (see fig. 7 and 8, p. 26 and 27).

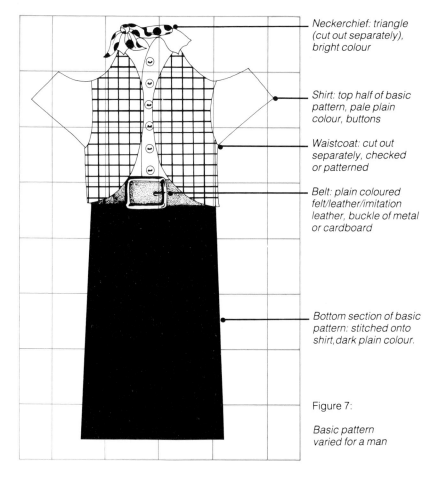

Neckerchief: triangle (cut out separately), bright colour

Shirt: top half of basic pattern, pale plain colour, buttons

Waistcoat: cut out separately, checked or patterned

Belt: plain coloured felt/leather/imitation leather, buckle of metal or cardboard

Bottom section of basic pattern: stitched onto shirt, dark plain colour.

Figure 7:

Basic pattern varied for a man

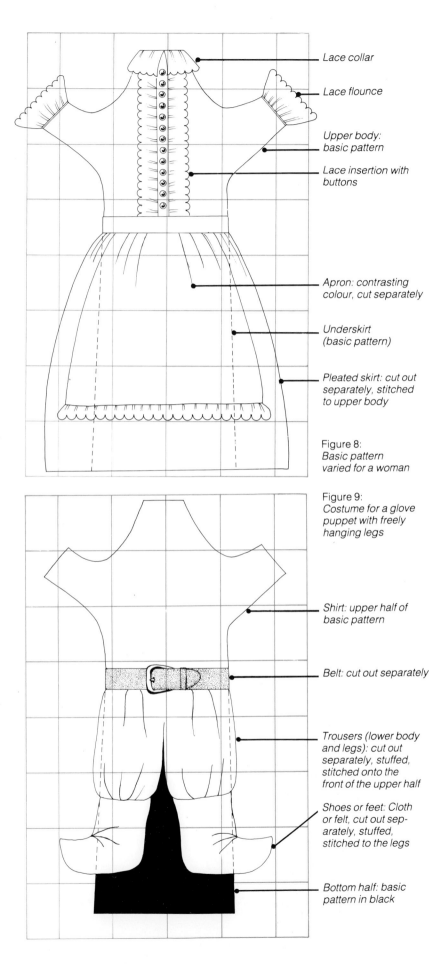

Lace collar

Lace flounce

Upper body:
basic pattern

Lace insertion with
buttons

Apron: contrasting
colour, cut separately

Underskirt
(basic pattern)

Pleated skirt: cut out
separately, stitched
to upper body

Figure 8:
Basic pattern
varied for a woman

Figure 9:
Costume for a glove
puppet with freely
hanging legs

Shirt: upper half of
basic pattern

Belt: cut out separately

Trousers (lower body
and legs): cut out
separately, stuffed,
stitched onto the
front of the upper half

Shoes or feet: Cloth
or felt, cut out sep-
arately, stuffed,
stitched to the legs

Bottom half: basic
pattern in black

Costume for glove puppet with legs

- Make a petticoat (body) from a simple fabric such as unbleached calico according to fig. 6 on p. 26.
- Make a costume with the bottom part in black.
- Cut the lower half of the body, legs and feet out of material of another colour (see fig. 9, p. 27). Stuff lightly.
- Sew the lower part of the body, legs and feet to the costume.

HANDS FOR A GLOVE PUPPET

For animal characters, the hands (forefeet) can be cut in one piece with the costume and a contrasting colour cloth can be sewn or stuck onto the front (see fig. 10, p. 28). For human figures, you can cut a simple hand with only a distinct thumb (see fig. 11, p. 28) or a more accurately shaped hand (see fig. 12.1. and 12.2, p 29) from felt or any suitable cloth. Cut out four hands and stitch two together to form a single hand. Turn right side out and stick or sew to the costume.

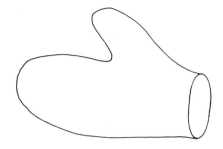

Figure 11:

Simple human hand with separate thumb

Figure 10.1:

Hands/forefeet/ wings of animal characters: cut in one with costume (basic pattern)

Contrasting colour cloth or felt

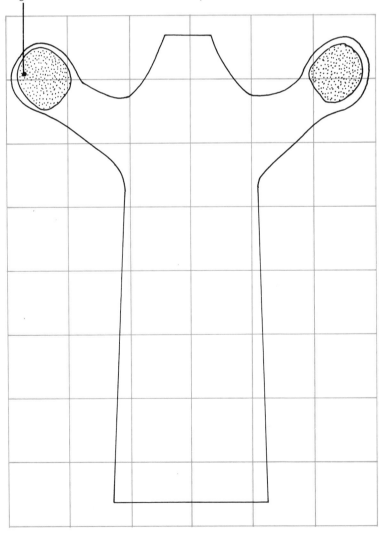

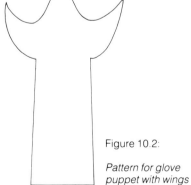

Figure 10.2:

Pattern for glove puppet with wings

28

The worm is made from a sock. The puppeteer moves it directly with his hands, covered with black gloves. The lion is made from a double sock (see p. 32). For the cat, the sock is replaced by ordinary cloth. (Made by Marie Kruger and Ruby Keyser)

Figure 12.1:

Shaped human hand with 5 fingers

Figure 12.2:

Shaped human hand with 4 fingers

Four glove puppets with moveable mouths: lion made out of polystyrene (see p. 33), giraffe made from foam rubber (see p. 33) and donkey and frog made out of cardboard and starched paper (see p. 33). (Made by drama students, U.S.)

GLOVE PUPPETS WITH MOVEABLE MOUTHS

These puppets are especially suitable for animal characters.

Sock puppet made out of a single sock

- Fold the toe section of the sock over to form a mouth (see fig. 13, p. 31).
- Stitch the folded section firmly around the mouth opening.
- If the sock does not come to the puppeteer's elbow, lengthen it from the neck section with material of a suitable colour and texture.

Decoration

Embroider eyes or use buttons. Embroider a black tip for the nose if necessary. Line the mouth with red or pink material. Sew on ears, legs, horns, etc., made from any suitable material or stuffed cloth. Make a mane (if necessary) from wool, string, raffia or strips of cloth. Cut spots, speckles and stripes from felt or any other material. Stick or stitch on.

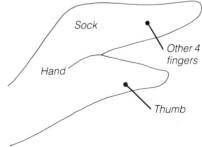

Figure 13:

Fold the sock back to form a mouth.

Sock puppet made from a pair of socks

- Pull one sock over the other.
- Fold the toe sections over to form a mouth.
- Stitch the folded section firmly around the mouth opening.
- Stuff the nose and head with cotton wool, or cut a piece of foam rubber into the required shape with a pair of scissors. The cotton wool or foam rubber is placed in the outside sock.
- Lengthen the sock, if necessary, as for the sock puppet made from a single sock.

Decoration

Follow the method as for only one sock.

Make a similar puppet by substituting ordinary material cut into three sections (see fig. 14.1, p. 32) and stitched together (see fig. 14.2, p. 32) for the sock(s).

Figure 14.1:

Cut parts 1 and 2 out of the same colour cloth.
Parts 3 forms the inside of the mouth.

Parts 1 and 2

Part 3

Part 1
Part 2
Part 3

Figure 14.2:

Parts 1, 2 and 3 fastened together to form a sock

Moveable mouth made from a cardboard box

- Cut the box open on three sides (top and sides).
- Fold so that the fourth side forms the join between the upper and lower jaws (see fig. 15, p. 32).
- Cover the cardboard box with cloth, unbleached calico or hessian to strengthen it, or paint it.
- Make a sock (i.e. neck or neck and body) out of material and stick it to the moveable jaws.

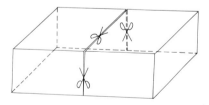

Figure 15:

Moveable jaws formed from a cardboard box
Cardboard: 3 sides are cut open.
The fourth side joins the jaws.

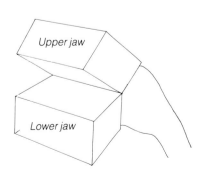

Upper jaw

Lower jaw

Decoration

Follow the method as for the one-sock puppet. If you make the neck and body out of unbleached calico or hessian, it can be painted. Decorate this simple, non-realistic puppet imaginatively. It is most suitable for younger children.

Moveable mouth made from starched paper/ foam rubber/ polystyrene

This construction method is suitable for animal and fantasy figures.

Starched paper

- Cut the upper and lower jaws separately out of thick cardboard.
- Prepare starch and newspaper as in construction of balloon base (see p. 22).
- Use starched pieces of paper to form the lower and upper jaw (nose section).
- Allow to dry and paint, or spread with paste or glue and cover with cloth.
- Join the upper and lower jaws with a strip of cloth pasted or glued on firmly.
- With a bent piece of cardboard, make a space for the thumb on the lower jaw. Stick or staple it on. Make a similar space for the other four figures on the upper jaw (see fig. 16, p. 33).
- Make a sock out of e.g. unbleached calico which fits over the hand and reaches to the elbow.
- Stick the sock to the jaws.
- Choose material of the appropriate colour and texture for the costume.
- Cut the costume wider than the sock to leave room for a stuffed head and so that it will suggest a suitable neck and front part of the body. In the case of e.g. a frog, the whole body can be represented. Gather the bottom end of the costume in with elastic and lengthen it with black cloth to cover the whole forearm.
- Attach with paste or glue to the moveable jaws.
- Stuff the head with cotton wool or a shaped piece of foam rubber.

Foam rubber

- Cut the jaws out of cardboard (see starched paper, p. 33), and then further shape them with foam rubber. Cut a space for the thumb in the foam rubber of the lower jaw, and a space for the other four fingers in the upper jaw.
- Continue by following the construction method given for starched paper.
  OR:
- Omit the cardboard base.
- Cut the foam rubber into the desired shape with a pair of sharp scissors.
- Cut out the necessary manipulation spaces for the fingers.
- Join the two jaws with a strong piece of cloth or felt which fills the whole inside of the mouth.

Polystyrene

- Follow one of the two methods given for foam rubber to shape the moveable jaws. Use a sharp knife, a file and sandpaper as tools. If you are going to paint the jaws, preferably cover the polystyrene with two layers of starched paper (see balloon base, p. 22) to strengthen it. First allow it to dry thoroughly and then paint.

Decoration

It is preferable to use three-dimensional eyes (buttons, table tennis balls, marbles, etc.). Make teeth out of stiff cardboard, foam rubber or layers of felt stuck together. For whiskers, you can use pipecleaners, string or wool. Embroider or paint the tip of the nose black (if necessary) or use a button. For a mane and forelegs, see the sock puppet, p. 31.

Figure 16.2:

Space in the lower jaw for the thumb

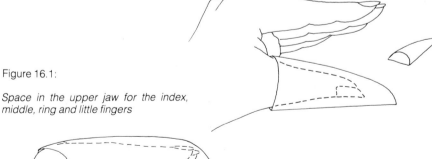

Figure 16.1:

Space in the upper jaw for the index, middle, ring and little fingers

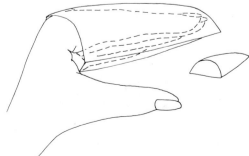

ROD PUPPETS

Rod puppets can be two-dimensional (flat figures) or three-dimensional. Flat figures are simple and quick to make, but as simplified puppets their performance capabilities are limited. Nevertheless children do enjoy enacting simple stories, verses and songs with them and they can come in very handy as the less important figures in an otherwise three-dimensional presentation.

Flat figure made from cardboard

- Trace the outlines of the figure on stiff cardboard. Decide whether the figure (e.g. person or animal) be full-face or in profile. Choose simple, clear outlines.

- Cut out the figure and decorate it.
- Attach a thin piece of wood or stiff wire to the back (see fig. 17, p. 34).

Decoration

Use paint or stick on any suitable material. The eyes (buttons, etc.), nose (cork, etc.) and hair (wool, string, raffia) can be three-dimensional.

Wooden spoon puppet

- Paint or stick a face on the rounded back of the spoon.
- Stick on hair (wool, cotton-wool, raffia, string).
- Stick a strip of felt or cloth just below the face to form a neck.
- Stick or sew a costume (e.g. a circular piece of material with a hole) to the neck.

Rod puppet without shoulder piece

- Use a polystyrene ball or any of the heads described for the ordinary glove puppet. Omit the neck cylinder.
- Put dowelling (round stick available at any hardware shop) approximately 1 cm wide and 50 cm long into the head.
- Stick a strip of felt or cloth just below the head to form a neck.
- Stick or sew a costume (circular piece of material) to the neck.
- If desired, simple arms can be made as follows: sew or stick a strip of the same material as used for the costume on either side of it and tie it at the "hand". Stitch a lightweight, stiff wire or small stick to the arms in order to manipulate them.

Decoration

Decorate the head as described for the ball head,
p. 20.

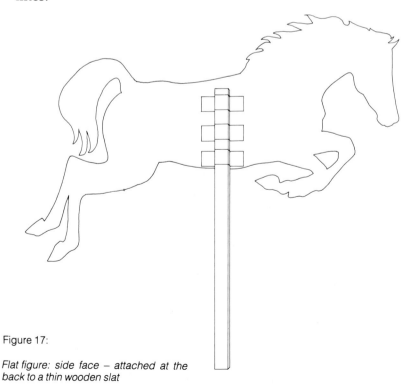

Figure 17:

Flat figure: side face – attached at the back to a thin wooden slat

The cow narrator and the piglet are rod puppets with moveable mouths. The heads are made of foam rubber and covered with stretch material. The puppeteers are unobtrusively dressed in black. (Made by education students, U.S.)

Rod puppet with simple shoulder piece

- Make and decorate a head as described for the ordinary glove puppet. Omit the neck cylinder.
- Take a toothpaste box (or similar cardboard box) and make two small holes by cutting crosses in it (see fig. 18, p. 37).
- Insert dowelling (approximately 1 cm x 50 cm) through the holes in the cardboard box to serve as the manipulating rod. Leave enough space (about 18 cm) at the top of the stick for a neck and to reach into the head.
- Attach the cardboard box to the stick with sticky tape, string or a strong strip of cloth. A small wooden triangle can be substituted for the cardboard box. Bore a hole through the piece of wood. Place in position and attach as for the cardboard box. If preferred, you can wind foam rubber round the piece of wood to give it more of a shape.
- Stick a strip of felt or cloth just above the shoulder piece (cardboard box or wooden block) to form a neck.
- Make a costume to represent the body. You can adapt the pattern for the glove puppet (see fig. 6, 7 and 8, p. 26 and 27). Extend the arms and sew on the hands. Shorten the neck if necessary.

Rod puppets (modelling-clay base and shoulder-pieces) from a performance of Aladdin's lamp. (Made by Leon Debliquy)

Figure 18:

Cut 2 crosses in a toothpaste box to form holes for the control rod (dowelling).

- Attach a piece of stiff wire (approximately 20 cm) to each hand.
- Put the costume over the shoulder piece.
- Attach the head to the top end of the dowelling.

FINGER PUPPETS

These miniature puppets can be made from a variety of materials: felt, cloth, the fingers of gloves, wool (knitted or crocheted) and cardboard. An elastic material allows the greatest degree of movement for the finger which must move the finger puppet. Cardboard is not very flexible and wears out quickly. It is, however, cheap and freely available.

Finger puppets made from the fingers of gloves, felt or cloth

- Cut the finger off the glove, or
- Substitute felt or cloth for the glove finger. Copy its shape and follow the same method.
- Cut a circle for the head from any suitable material. Tack around the circle, gather up and stuff lightly with cotton wool. Fit it over the end of the glove finger and stitch on.
- Stick, paint or embroider the face (eyes, nose, mouth).
- Attach hair (wool, raffia, string, fringes, etc.).

Knitted finger puppet

- Choose an appropriate colour 4-ply wool for the head and another colour wool for the body.

- Cast on 14 stitches on a no. 12 knitting needle.
- Knit approximately 24 rows of ribbing for the body.
- Knit approximately 8 rows of stocking stitch for the head. Do not cast off.
- Thread a needle with a strand of wool (the same colour as the head). Lift the stitches off the knitting needle with the threaded needle. Pull tightly together and sew firmly at the top of the head.
- Sew the knitted section together to form a finger cylinder and turn right side out.
- Stuff the head with cotton-wool.
- Use a double strand of wool and a needle to pull in the "neck". Wind the strand of wool tightly round the neck and work a few stitches through the neck.
- Embroider the face (eyes, nose, mouth).
- Use wool for the hair, moustache and beard (if applicable).
- If necessary, knit two thin strips of ribbing for the arms and attach them to the body.

A friendly witch (balloon base) with her cat (finger puppet made of cloth), an elf (glove puppet with freely hanging legs – see p. 22, 38 and 27) and King Redbeard (balloon base) under a tree (cloth draped over wood). (Made by drama students, U.S.)

MARIONETTES

Marionettes can be highly sophisticated puppets which are manipulated from above by many strings. Less skilful people can make a simple construction with fewer control strings and still entertain their audience.

Marionette made from cardboard

- Study fig. 19 on p. 42 and collect the following cardboard boxes (or similar ones):
  head: three round cheese boxes stuck on top of each other or a square box (at least as wide as the neck)
  neck: half an empty toilet roll
  body: empty oats box
  arms: two empty toilet rolls per arm
  legs: two empty tinfoil rolls (halved)
  hands: cardboard
  feet: cardboard
- Paint each section and allow to dry
- Attach the different parts loosely to one another with strong thread or string. Staple or stick the hands and feet to the rest of the figure.
- Decorate the face. For a three-dimensional quality, you should use buttons or lids for the eyes and a cork or lid for the nose. Use wool, string, raffia, etc. for hair.

Marionettes from a performance of the fairy-tale The Princess and the Sea Monster *(Made by education students, U.S.)*

- Stick two wooden slats together to form a cross. This forms the control bar.
- Attach the controlling strings (double cotton thread) as follows to the marionette and the control bar (see fig. 19, p. 42): one to either side of the head and connected to the top slat, one to each forearm and connected to the lower slat, one to each upper leg (just above the "knee") and connected to the lower slat of the control bar.

Human figure made from material

- Use any material (e.g. wool jersey, stockings) which is easily shaped, durable and of the right weight, i.e. light enough for the puppeteer to lift and manipulate the marionette, and not so light that the puppeteer has little control over movements.
- Study fig. 20 on p. 43. The natural proportions of the human body are not imitated. The marionette's head, hands and feet are larger and its legs slightly shorter for greater visual expression. A size of about 40-50 cm will be easily manageable.
- Cut the following pieces from the material: head, body or head and body in one piece, two arms with hands, two legs with feet.
- Stuff each part with cotton-wool, cut-up stockings, small pieces of foam rubber, etc.
- Tie off the head with a thin piece of string if head and body is cut in one piece.
- Tie off each arm at the

"elbow" and "wrist".
- Tie off each leg at the "knee" and foot.
- Stitch the head, body, arms and legs lightly but firmly together.
- If you wish, you can make a costume for the marionette.
- Decorate the face with eyes (painted, buttons, beads), nose (painted, button, shaping with needle and thread), chin (optional, shaping with needle and thread, cheeks (optional, shaping with needle and thread), and hair (wool, string, raffia).
- Attach two wooden slats to form a cross. This forms the control bar.

- Attach the control strings (a double thread of cotton) as follows to the marionette and control bar (see fig. 20, p. 43): one to either side of the head and connected to the top slat of the control bar, one to each hand and connected to the lower slat, one to each upper leg (just above the "knee") and connected to the lower slat of the control bar.

Animal figure made from cloth

- Choose suitable cloth (see human figure on p. 43).

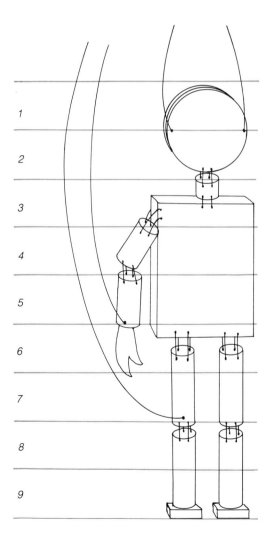

Figure 19:

Marionette made from cardboard containers

42

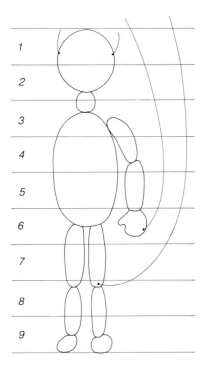

Figure 20:

Marionette (human figure) made from stretch material

Figure 21:

A marionette with 4 control strings and two separate control bars

- Cut out the animal's head, body, four legs and tail separately.
- Stitch each part, stuff and sew up.
- Attach the different parts lightly to each other.
- Decorate the face.
- Attach a control string to each side of the head and connect to a straight wooden slat (see fig. 21, p. 43).
- Attach one control string to the centre of the back and one control string to the tip of the tail. Connect the two strings to a straight wooden slat (see fig. 21). (The control bar therefore consists of two separate slats: one for the head, and one for the body and tail.)

SHADOW PUPPETS

These traditionally two-dimensional figures cut from wood or leather are of Oriental origin. You can safely use stiff cardboard. It is cheap, freely available and very effective. The success of a shadow puppet depends on simple, clear outlines without unnecessary detail and with strong emphasis, even exaggeration, of the characteristic form. You can even cut out sections of the solid figure to allow light through. This not only gives a more decorative figure, but provides necessary detail. A simple shadow puppet has no moveable arms, legs or head. More skilled puppeteers can manipulate these parts with thin sticks or wires.

Simple shadow puppet

- Trace the side-view outlines of the figure onto stiff cardboard.
- Cut the figure out.
- Stick a thin piece of wire, a knitting needle, sosatie stick or thin piece of wood to the figure.

Decoration

No decoration is necessary. Even if the cardboard is not black, it will throw a dark shadow on the screen because it does not allow any light through. For a more decorative figure, you can cut out sections before attaching the wire or stick (see fig. 23, p. 44). You can stick coloured cellophane over these openings. Always keep a clear, unbroken outline.

Shadow puppet with moveable parts

- Draw the different parts of the figure (e.g. head, body, arms, legs) on stiff cardboard. These moveable parts must be designed to overlap when you attach them (see fig. 22, p. 44).
- Cut out the different parts.
- Attach the parts of the puppet with cotton which is firmly knotted on both sides, or use split pins.
- Stick a small strip of wood or some stiff wire to the central section of the body so that the shadow puppets can be held vertically.
- Attach strings, thin strips of wood or wires to the other moveable parts.

Decoration

Follow the method described for the simple shadow puppet, p. 43.

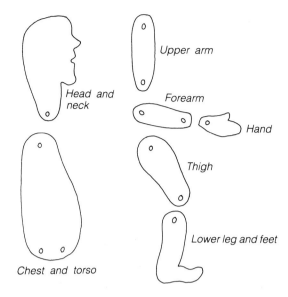

Head and neck

Upper arm

Forearm

Hand

Thigh

Lower leg and feet

Chest and torso

Figure 22:

Different parts of the human body overlap for a shadow puppet with moveable limbs. Attach the parts to each other with split pins.

Figure 23:

Shadow puppets: a giraffe with the spots cut out to allow light through

CHAPTER 5

How to animate the puppet

The puppet is a lifeless object which is animated mainly by movement, supplemented by speech.

Make the puppet move like this

Because the puppet is a lifeless object, the puppeteer must make it move to give it "life" and to entertain the audience. A puppet is never complete before it has moved with the help of an imaginative puppeteer.

General hints

- Make the puppet move from place to place with the help of finger, wrist and arm movements (separately and combined). The strength and tempo of these movements are determined by the character and emotions of the puppet and by the situation.
- Every type of puppet has certain typical movements. Yet the movements of two puppets of the same kind are never identical. Always try to find movements which are typical of your puppet's character.
- Try to find meaningful, clear and economical movements which are both simple and imaginative.
- Guard against the continual repetition of the same movement, e.g. swinging arms or a nodding head. Typical movements must still be meaningful and hold the audience's attention with their variety and imaginativeness.
- Limit movement as far as possible to the puppet which is speaking. A puppet often does not have a moveable mouth. Another kind of movement must therefore indicate to the audience who is speaking. When the other puppets are standing still, they must look as if they are alive by listening to what is said and looking at what is done.
- Pay attention to the posture of the puppet. It must not bend sideways, forwards or backwards without reason. This betrays clumsiness or fatigue on the part of the puppeteer.

The middle glove puppet has the correct neutral posture, while the glove puppet on the left is leaning backwards and the glove puppet on the right is at an angle. (Made by education students, U.S.)

- When the puppet is standing up or walking it must always remain on the same acting level. Just as a marionette cannot fly through the air or give at the knees without reason, so a puppet which is manipulated from below cannot just disappear or sink lower.

Pay attention to the height at which the puppet moves. The glove puppet in the middle is at the right height, while the one on the left is lifted too high and the puppeteer's arm is visible. Only the head and upper body of the glove puppet on the right are visible.

- Lift the puppet slightly higher if it stands or exits at the back of the acting area. It will then seem to the audience as if the puppet is staying at the same height.
- The puppet is usually smaller than a living person or animal and is never true to life. Its way of moving should just remind the audience of a particular kind of person or animal. It must move freely within its fantasy nature and not try to perform realistic movements. For this reason its movements can sometimes be bold and exaggerated if the situation justifies it.

- Group puppets meaningfully in a scene. Do not have them all standing in a row in front. Vary the grouping by making the puppet move around. Pay careful attention to the placing of the main character.
- In traditional puppetry only the puppet is visible. If a part of the puppeteer (head, arm, hand) suddenly becomes visible, it destroys the fantasy. Visible parts of the body should be covered with black material.
- A puppeteer may stand, kneel or sit when he is manipulating a puppet from below. The standing position is best because it allows the puppeteer and his puppet to move easily. The kneeling and sitting positions, especially in the case of a group, easily lead to a static quality and fewer changes in the grouping.

A scene from The Wizard's Wicked Plan *with the main character logically in the middle. The puppets are looking at each other and do not turn towards the audience when they are in conversation. The wizard's slave takes no part in the discussion and therefore stands behind the main character. (Made by drama students, U.S.)*

which the hand feels most comfortable and which allows for the best manipulation.

- The movements of the puppeteer's fingers make the glove puppet's head and arms move, while his wrist movements move the puppet's body. The puppeteer should preferably always stay directly below his puppet.

From a standing position, the puppeteers can not only group the puppets meaningfully, but also move around easily in order to prevent them from being visually static.

Hints for specific puppets

Ordinary glove puppet

- The glove puppet is manipulated from below by the puppeteer putting his hand in the sock, i.e. costume or body, of the glove puppet and stretching his arm/forearm vertically upwards.
- The puppeteer's fingers can be placed inside the glove puppet in various different ways (see fig. 24, p. 46). Always choose the position in

- Certain movements and emotions which often feature in glove puppetry are carried out as follows:

Walking: *Rotate your wrist lightly and rhythmically from side to side or up and down while keeping the puppet's head erect.*

Jumping: *Make an upward semicircular movement with your arm.*

Falling: *Use a large arm movement and even a semicircular movement of the wrist to make the puppet fall suddenly. Before making this movement, hold the puppet motionless for a moment to create the right rhythm.*

Affirmation: *Move your finger backwards and forwards in the puppet's head, and combine this with a similar wrist movement if it signifies very strong agreement.*

Denial: *Rotate your wrist around an imaginary vertical axis.*

Greeting: *Either of the puppet's arms may be waved. This movement is usually clearer if the arm which is not being used is held away from the puppet's body.*

Thinking: *The puppet taps or scratches its head lightly with one hand, or crosses its hands and then taps lightly on one hand with the other.*

Fright: *Bend the puppet's head slightly backwards and lift up its arms, or clap both hands over its face. (Surprise can be expressed in the same way.)*

Bowing: *The puppeteer drops his wrist forwards, causing the puppet to bend from the waist. To make the movement elegant and courteous, one of the puppet's hands is pressed to its body.*

Figure 24:

Different positions in which the puppeteer can place his hands inside the glove puppet

The clowns are thinking of a plan. The one on the left lightly taps his own head. His friend on the right crosses his hands and taps with one hand on the other. (Made by Marie Kruger and an education student, U.S.)

The queen bows before the angry king: the puppeteer flicks his wrist forward and holds one of the queen's hands elegantly against her cloak. (Made by education students, U.S.)

The Westerner and the Chinaman get a fright when they see each other. The Westerner throws his head back and raises his arms. The Chinaman claps his hands over his face. (Made by Miki Redelinghuys)

Glove puppet with a moveable mouth

- Place your thumb in the lower jaw and the other four fingers in the upper jaw in order to move them. The mouth, as in actual speech, is always open for vowels. The puppet's mouth should be opened very wide for emphasized words. For less important words, only a slight movement is sometimes visible. For neat and intelligible speech, the mouth should be properly closed for consonants and less important words. The same technique is used for singing. When a puppet is holding a long note, the mouth must be very wide open.
- Use wrist movements to move the rest of the puppet's head.
- Move the puppet's body using your wrist and arm.
- As for the ordinary glove puppet, you can stretch your arm/forearm vertically upwards, but your wrist must be bent slightly forwards to make the puppet's face, and particularly its eyes, visible to the audience. In the case of some animal characters, you should bend your arm horizontally at the elbow.
- For animal characters, the legs can simply dangle.

The lion's face is clearly visible because the puppeteer's wrist is bent forward. The other puppeteer bends his forearm and wrist backwards while the giraffe sings a long note. (Made by education students, U.S.)

49

When you move your wrist and arm to manipulate the puppet's neck and body, the dangling legs will in fact move to a certain extent. In the case of human characters, you should move the arms with rods like those of a conventional rod puppet.

Rod puppet

- When using a booth or screen, hold the rod puppet upright with a central control bar. The height of the booth and the puppeteers will, as in the case of the preceding puppets, determine whether the puppeteers should stretch the whole arm or only the forearm vertically upwards.
- When the puppeteer is not concealed from the audience, he should hold the puppet directly in front of him. Puppeteers can be unobtrusively dressed in black or wear costumes which go with the text and with the costumes of the puppets in the play, so that the text is presented by both puppets and living actors.
- Use your weaker hand to hold the central control bar and your stronger hand to manipulate the control rods for the hands because the latter demands greater skill.
- Hold the control rods for the hands lightly with the ends resting in the palm of your hand. The index, middle, ring and little fingers hold the rods while you use your thumb to move the rods apart from each other if e.g. the puppet opens its arms wide or just moves one of its hands.

- For neat, dexterous manipulation you should keep your eyes on the puppet's hands and not on your own fingers.
- Sometimes one control rod for the hands can hang freely when the puppet is not speaking. The other hand is then slightly raised.

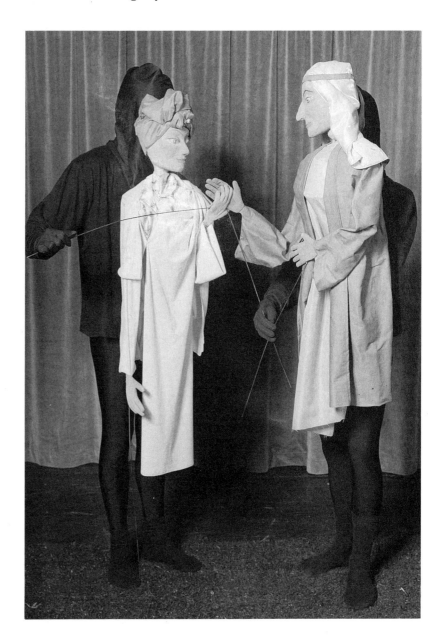

The visible players (dressed in black) hold the rod puppets directly before them and handle the arm rods with the stronger hand. One of the female puppet's arm rods hangs freely while the male puppet speaks to her and therefore uses both his hands. (Made by education students, U.S.)

Finger puppet

- As the name indicates, the finger puppet is pulled over the puppeteer's finger/s.
- Cover one hand with a black glove and then put the puppet over your finger.
- Puppeteers usually find the middle or the index finger the most comfortable.
- Turn the palm or back of the hand upwards, downwards or horizontally towards the audience, depending on which position is the easiest and most comfortable.
- When you manipulate more than one finger puppet, you can put all the puppets on the fingers of the same hand or use the fingers of both hands. This will depend on the action to be performed.

Shadow puppet

- The shadow puppet can be manipulated from more than one position: from below, from the sides and even from above.
- Make sure that the puppeteers never come between the shadow puppets and the light source.
- All movements must be subtle and meaningful.
- Hold the rods lightly in order to carry out delicate movements as precisely as possible.
- Reverse movements (i.e. when the shadow puppet walks back to the place from which it came) should be carried out rapidly so that the puppet only disappears momentarily.
- Slow, simple but imagina-tive movements are ideal.
- Move the shadow puppet up close to the screen for a clear image.

Marionette

- The marionette is always manipulated from above with the puppeteer standing on a higher level (e.g. a chair, table, bridge, etc.).
- Keep your eye on the marionette, not on the control bar and strings.

The marionette is always manipulated from above. The puppeteer keeps his eye on the marionette and not on the control mechanisms. Co-ordinate the right leg and the left arm and conversely. (Made by education students, U.S.)

- Movements need not be completely realistic. Accept, for instance, the strange walking action as part of the marionette and make it part of the characterization.
- For the walking action you must pull the leg strings quickly with the free hand and turn the control bar in the opposite direction from the swing of the marionette to prevent an exaggerated sideways swing.
- Co-ordinate the arms and legs: the right arm and left leg work together, and vice versa.
- Combine arm movements, slight head movements, small steps and a slight bending of the body when the marionette is speaking.

How to make the puppet "speak"

The dialogue or narrative can be handled in various ways. Record it beforehand on tape, speak it yourself during the performance, or have someone else who is not handling a puppet do the talking.

A tape recording, however, leads to certain static qualities in the puppetry, because it leaves no room for audience participation or reaction. Just like dialogue which is being handled by someone other than the manipulator himself, it requires very precise synchronization with the movements. Try rather to have each manipulator handling his own dialogue. In the case of children it gives them an opportunity to improve their language and speech skills, to be creative in more than one area and to acquire more self-confidence.

Speech hints

- Breathe deeply, because without breath you cannot produce a sufficiently audible voice.
- Speak clearly. The tongue, lips and lower jaw must move quickly and easily.
- Vary the tempo according to the requirements of the text. Portray character distinctions with the help of differences in tempo.
- Handle vocal transformations carefully so that they never place any stress on the voice. Avoid strained extremes of pitch. They sound false and affected, lead to inaudible and incomprehensible speech and can damage the vocal cords. Remember that the gender, age and appearance of the puppeteer are not visible to the audience. Work therefore rather with suggestion as far as vocal transformation goes. Instead of changing the natural pitch of the voice, you can use differences such as a nasal voice, a lisp, a burr, a stammer, different accents and regional pronunciation.

CHAPTER 6

Acting areas

Traditionally, the puppeteer is always fully or at least partly concealed from the audience. In modern puppetry the puppeteer is often visible, but once the audience is absorbed by the puppet show it quickly forgets about the visible manipulator.

Children puppeteers usually prefer to be concealed from the audience. This not only lets the shy child feel freer, but gives everyone a feeling of excitement, healthy seriousness, dedication and a wonderful awareness that they are all making theatre.

Permanent acting areas can be very sophisticated, but simple acting areas are also effective and can quickly be created from furniture or other apparatus at hand.

Ideas for instant acting areas

- *Perform above the closed lower half of a door.*
- *Stretch a rope across a doorway and throw a sheet or tablecloth over it.*
- *Stretch a rope between two walls and throw a cloth over it.*
- *Put a long-handled duster or plank across the backs of two chairs and throw a cloth over it.*
- *Turn a table on its side and sit or kneel behind it for glove, rod and finger puppets. Stand upright behind the table and let your marionette hang over it from above.*
- *Cut a little window in a large cardboard box. If it is high enough, one or two players can stand inside. Otherwise place it on a table. Suitable for glove, rod and finger puppets.*

Proscenium puppet booth

This booth (see fig. 25, p. 53) is suitable for any type of puppet which is controlled from below. For shadow puppets, thick tracing paper or sheeting is stretched tightly over the opening. Because of limited space it can only be used by a small group of puppeteers at a time.

- Make the wooden framework (three frames) from light pine slats.
- Stretch cloth or unbleached calico over the framework and nail down. Paint the calico.
- Nail a light curtain track to the slat just above the opening and make small curtains.
- Join the three wooden frames with hinges.

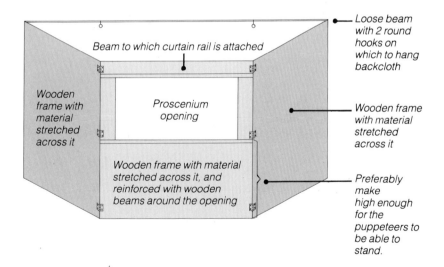

Labels on figure:
Beam to which curtain rail is attached
Loose beam with 2 round hooks on which to hang backcloth
Wooden frame with material stretched across it
Proscenium opening
Wooden frame with material stretched across it
Wooden frame with material stretched across it, and reinforced with wooden beams around the opening
Preferably make high enough for the puppeteers to be able to stand.

Figure 25:

Proscenium booth for puppets which are manipulated from below

Simple open puppet booth

This booth (see fig. 26, p. 54) is suitable for glove, rod, finger and shadow puppets. Make a loose shadow screen (see fig. 24, p. 47) and attach firmly with clamps. This booth can have a diameter of approximately 1,7-2,0 m and is ideal for a larger group of puppeteers.

- Make the wooden framework out of light pine slats. It must be high enough for the puppeteers to be able to stand while manipulating the puppets.
- Stretch cloth or unbleached calico across it (paint it after it has been stretched onto the framework).
- Join the framework with hinges.
- Optional: Make a stand from light pine or other wood with sturdy, heavy feet (see fig. 27, p. 54). It must be higher than the booth. Hook a backcloth (black or painted with a scene) onto the stand.

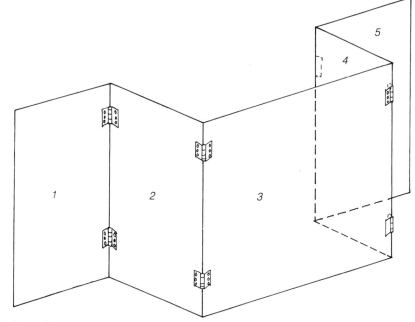

Figure 26:

Simple open booth made from 5 screens attached to each other with hinges. Screens 1 and 5 can be left out. Make the screens high enough for the puppeteers to be able to stand behind them.

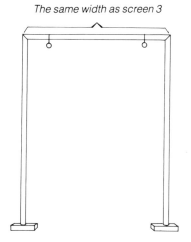

The same width as screen 3

Figure 27:

A stand on which to hang the backcloth, ± 1 m higher than the booth

Acting area made with screens of different heights

This type of acting area for glove and rod puppets (see fig. 28, p. 54) consists of two or more screens and creates an open booth with more depth. The different screens can also be used for a rapid change of scene.

Figure 28:

An open acting area with screens of different heights

Marionette theatre with proscenium opening

In this acting area the players are completely concealed from the audience.

- Make three screens (see fig. 29, p. 55) of the same height out of light pine slats. The central screen has an opening (see fig. 29.2A, p. 55) through which the marionettes are visible. It must be high enough to leave space for a stage (see fig. 29.4, p. 55), making the marionette easily visible to the audience and concealing the puppeteers standing on the bridge (see fig. 29.3, p. 55). Use light pine slats for the framework and light plywood for the stage. Paint the floor black, or cover with black cloth or unbleached calico painted black.
- Make the bridge (see fig. 29.4, p. 55) as follows: Use sturdy wooden beams and planks to make a platform on which the puppeteers can stand. Make two wooden railings. Attach one to the front of the bridge so that the puppeteers can rest their arms on it. Screw two hooks into it so that the backcloth can hang from it. Attach one railing to the back of the bridge to prevent the puppeteers from stepping too far backwards and falling from the bridge.

This acting area therefore consists of three parts:

- *screens attached to each other with hinges,*
- *a stage on which the marionettes move, and*
- *a bridge on which the puppeteers stand.*

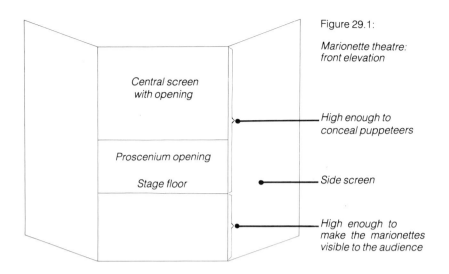

Figure 29.1:

Marionette theatre: front elevation

Central screen with opening

Proscenium opening

Stage floor

High enough to conceal puppeteers

Side screen

High enough to make the marionettes visible to the audience

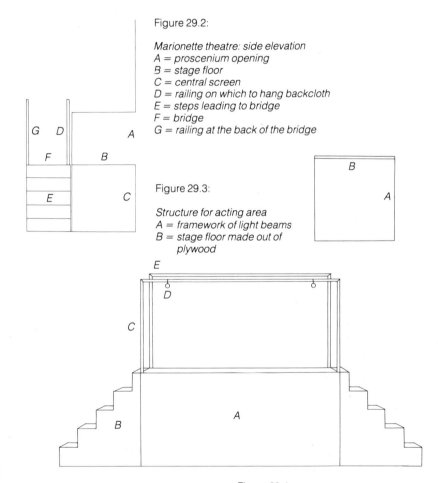

Figure 29.2:

Marionette theatre: side elevation
A = proscenium opening
B = stage floor
C = central screen
D = railing on which to hang backcloth
E = steps leading to bridge
F = bridge
G = railing at the back of the bridge

Figure 29.3:

Structure for acting area
A = framework of light beams
B = stage floor made out of plywood

Figure 29.4:

Bridge with steps and railings
A = platform for puppeteers to stand on
B = steps screwed onto A
C = wooden railing screwed onto A for armrest and backcloth
D = hooks in wooden railing on which to hang backcloth
E = wooden railing at the back of A to prevent puppeteers from stepping too far back

CHAPTER 7

Puppetry staging techniques

Décor

The nature of and need for décor is always determined by the text. Often puppetry can be carried out against a plain backcloth (e.g. black). Whenever you do use décor, stick to the following guidelines:

- Décor does not have to be realistic.
- Use symbols and the symbolic value of colours. A red cloth (backcloth or over the front screen) can suggest a palace, one or two trees can give the impression of a forest.
- The puppets and their manipulation should never be dominated by the décor.
- Always use lightweight material, e.g. cardboard, polystyrene, paper, paper and starch, cloth, etc.
- Scene changes must take place rapidly.

Lighting

It is essential that the puppets should always remain easily visible. This does not necessarily mean extra lighting. In daylight, as in the classroom for example, it is often unnecessary, seeing that the circumstances are informal and the puppets clearly visible. In more formal circumstances the light in the venue can be dimmed and the acting area lit. In daylight it is not always possible (or necessary) to darken the surroundings completely.

The simplest additional lighting is provided by two spotlights attached to stands and placed so that the acting area is lit crosswise. Put a light stand on each side of the acting area and turn the spotlight so that it illuminates the opposite side.

Although under many circumstances puppetry can do without lighting, lighting and darkening (even if not completely) are essential for shadow puppetry. Unlike other forms of puppetry, the light is placed behind the shadow screen. Place it in the centre so that it shines obliquely from above on the shadow screen. An overhead projector is an ideal light source for shadow puppetry and is available at most schools.

Sound

Like décor, sound effects do not always have to be completely realistic. Noises can be imitated in various ways. Puppeteers, particularly children, must be allowed to experiment with sound mimicry. These sound effects should, especially in the case of children, be produced behind the scenes to avoid the use of a tape recorder.

In rehearsing the puppetry, enough time must be allowed to practise the synchronization of the action and the sound effects. Sound effects should always be an essential part of the presentation. Events must therefore necessitate these effects.

Music before the opening scene or between the scenes can be recorded on tape or played live behind the scenes. The latter music will perhaps be simpler, but can give a player the opportunity to use his or her particular talent. At the same time it eliminates the embarrassment of a music tape which breaks at an untimely moment. Ensure that the mood of the music always fits in with the atmosphere of the puppet play.